BOOKS AND
FOR
READING
YOUNG FOLK

DONATED BY
SUNRISE ROTARY OF WEST BEND
IN HONOR OF
JEAN REED

FOCUS ON
FAMILY
MATTERS

Helping Hands:
How Families Can Reach Out to their Community

FOCUS ON FAMILY MATTERS

Focus on Family Matters

Helping Hands:
How Families Can Reach Out to their Community

Rich Mintzer

Marvin Rosen, Ph.D.
Consulting Editor

CHELSEA HOUSE
P U B L I S H E R S
A Haights Cross Communications Company
Philadelphia

CHELSEA HOUSE PUBLISHERS

EDITOR IN CHIEF Sally Cheney
DIRECTOR OF PRODUCTION Kim Shinners
CREATIVE MANAGER Takeshi Takahashi
MANUFACTURING MANAGER Diann Grasse

Staff for HELPING HANDS: HOW FAMILIES CAN REACH OUT TO THEIR COMMUNITY

ASSOCIATE EDITOR Bill Conn
PICTURE RESEARCHER Sarah Bloom
PRODUCTION ASSISTANT Jaimie Winkler
COVER AND SERIES DESIGNER Takeshi Takahashi
LAYOUT 21st Century Publishing and Communications, Inc.

A Haights Cross Communications ✦ Company

http://www.chelseahouse.com

First Printing

1 3 5 7 9 8 6 4 2

Library of Congress Cataloging-in-Publication Data
Mintzer, Richard.
  Helping hands : how families can reach out to their community /Richard Mintzer.
     p. cm.—(Focus on family matters)
Summary: Provides real-life examples of ways that young people and their families
can reach out as volunteers to help others cope with tragedies or just to make their
communities better places in which to live.
Includes bibliographical references and index.
  ISBN 0-7910-6952-4
  1. Voluntarism—United States—Juvenile literature. 2. Family—United States—
Juvenile literature. [1. Voluntarism.] I. Title. II. Series.
HN90.V64 M56 2002
302'.14—dc21

                                                          2002006783

Contents

Introduction

Marvin Rosen, Ph.D.
Consulting Editor

Bad things sometimes happen to good people. We've probably all heard that expression. But what happens when the "good people" are teenagers?

Growing up is stressful and difficult to negotiate. Teenagers are struggling to becoming independent, trying to cut ties with their families that they see as restrictive, burdensome, and unfair. Rather than attempting to connect in new ways with their parents, they may withdraw. When bad things do happen, this separation may make the teen feel alone in coping with difficult and stressful issues.

Focus on Family Matters provides teens with practical information about how to cope when bad things happen to them. The series deals foremost with feelings—the emotional pain associated with adversity. Grieving, fear, anger, stress, guilt, and sadness are addressed head on. Teens will gain valuable insight and advice about dealing with their feelings, and for seeking help when they cannot help themselves.

The authors in this series identify some of the more serious problems teens face. In so doing, they make three assumptions: First, teens who find themselves in difficult situations are not at fault and should not blame themselves. Second, teens can overcome difficult situations, but may need help to do so. Third, teens bond with their families, and the strength of this bond influences their ability to handle difficult situations.

These books are also about communication—specifically about the value of communication. None of the problems covered occurs in a vacuum, and none of the situations should be faced by anyone alone. Each either involves a close family member or affects the entire family. Since families teach teens how to trust, relate to others, and solve problems, teens need to bond with families to develop normally and become emotionally whole. Success in dealing with adversity depends not only on the strength of the individual teen, but also upon the resources of the family in providing support, advice, and material assistance. Strong attachment to care givers in a supporting, nurturing, safe family structure is essential to successful coping.

Some teens learn to cope with adversity—they absorb the pain, they adjust, and they go on. But for others, the trauma they experience seems like an insurmountable challenge—they become angry, stressed, and depressed. They may withdraw from friends, they may stop going to school, and their grades may slip. They may draw negative attention to themselves and express their pain and fear by rebelling. Yet, in each case, healing can occur.

The teens who cope well with adversity, who are able to put the past behind them and regain their momentum, are no less sensitive or caring than those who suffer most. Yet there is a difference. Teens who are more resilient to trauma are able to dig deep down into their own resources, to find strength in their families and in their own skills, accomplishments, goals, aspirations, and values. They are able to find reasons for optimism and to feel confidence in their capabilities. This series recognizes the effectiveness of these strategies, and presents problem-solving skills that every teen can use.

Focus on Family Matters is positive, optimistic, and supportive. It gives teens hope and reinforces the power of their own efforts to handle adversity. And most importantly, it shows teens that while they cannot undo the bad things that have happen, they have the power to shape their own futures and flourish as healthy, productive adults.

September 11th: It Changed All of Us

■ When Rebecca and her brother Eric were picked up early from grade school in Manhattan on Tuesday, September 11th, they, like many other children being taken out of school early by their parents, did not know what was going on. Parents sat with their children in the lobby of the school or they talked as they slowly headed home. They tried to find the right words to explain to their children what had happened downtown at the World Trade Center.

New York City was very different during the week after the terrorist attack. Emergency vehicles raced up and down the avenues, fighter planes flew overhead, and the line at the local blood center stretched down the block. Everyone had a story to tell about someone they knew who had either made it out or not. It was the only thing people talked about and it was on television all day and night.

By the following weekend, there were thousands of workers

and rescue crews digging through the rubble of what remained of the collapsed World Trade Center towers in lower Manhattan. The city was blanketed with posters of the thousands of people who were missing and feared lost in the debris. Everyone wanted to pitch in and help in some way. On Thursday, Rebecca and Eric's school planned a donation drive to collect food, blankets, clothing, and tools to send to the crews working downtown. That Sunday was the day of the collections for the donation drive. This school event was very different than other school activities for Eric and Rebecca. The principal showed up in jeans and a work shirt. Teachers, students, and parents collected boxes of items to donate to the workers. It was the first time Rebecca or Eric had seen the people in their school community in a different light. Suddenly they were not teachers, parents, and students, but volunteers working together to try and help in any small way they could after this horrible tragedy that shook their city and the world.

The tragic events of September 11, 2001 shocked and angered people all over the nation and throughout the world. It was a horrifying day that led to great sorrow as everyone felt deep sadness for the many victims of the horrible tragedy. It also left us all with many unanswered questions, such as: How could anyone do something so horrible to innocent people? How could something like this happen in our own country? Will America ever be safe again?

If you felt helpless and shed tears in the days and weeks after the events of September 11th, you were certainly not alone. Millions of people also felt great sadness, anger, and even frustration. Many people talked

The tragic attacks of September 11, 2001 have sparked a spirit of volunteerism in Americans across the nation. Intense events like these challenge us to put aside our personal differences and donate our help where it is most needed.

to counselors about how they felt. Others talked to friends, family, and even strangers in online chat rooms. It took weeks, even months before people went back to their daily routines, especially in New York City, where an estimated 3,000 people died at the World Trade Center as a result of the terrorist act. Everyone talked about how hard it was to believe that this had really happened and it made people think about how precious life really is. In addition, nearly everyone wanted to do something to pitch in and help.

During the months following the attack, many people changed how they thought about the world around them. In a land of great opportunity and rewards, Americans stopped thinking about their own personal gain and started focusing more attention on helping others. There was a desire to get involved and help people get through this terrible tragedy.

It is not uncommon for people who go through an intense situation together, such as the events of September 11th, to bond with each other and share their distress. The feeling that "We've all been through this together" prompts people to put aside their political and social differences and unite. In the aftermath of

How did you feel

when you heard about the September 11th terrorist attacks?

September 11th, **volunteers** from all walks of life were working side by side. Working together, people were also able to avoid the depression that might have set in if they did not keep busy.

The tragic acts of the terrorists killed thousands of people, but did not kill the spirit of Americans who will always be ready to help one and other whenever necessary.

And there were many people who needed a helping hand. Not only were there families of the victims needing support and assistance, but there were also many people who were out of work because their office or the company they worked for had been destroyed. Even businesses that were not located in the World Trade Center were affected. For example, there were fewer people flying after the attacks. As a result, thousands of people who worked for the airlines or in the travel industry also lost their jobs. A struggling economy, bordering on a **recession**, only got worse and October and November saw more and more people losing their jobs as the holiday season approached.

The outpouring of help and support for the victims, the rescue workers and the many people affected by the events of September 11th began immediately. Within hours after the hijacked airplanes struck the World Trade Center, people in New York City were lined up at the blood banks, ready to donate much-needed blood for those injured in the attacks. In fact, one blood center, on East 67th Street in Manhattan, drew such large crowds that they had to turn people away because they could no longer accommodate any more donors. The American Red Cross also set up a **command center** at the Chelsea Piers on the west side of Manhattan to take care of the injured. Many volunteers went to the piers to help in any way they could. Ironically, Chelsea Piers were the same piers that saw the survivors of the Titanic come ashore 89 years earlier.

In the days following the tragedy, several funds were set up to collect donations. The American Red Cross set up the Liberty Fund and created an emergency grant program for the families of the victims of the attacks,

Hours after reports of the World Trade Center disaster hit the news media, people all over New York City looked for ways to help. Some restaurants closed their doors to regular customers and began providing free food for rescue workers.

providing cash that families needed for housing, food, medical care, and other immediate needs. Numerous other funds were started, including The New York State World Trade Center Relief Fund and The September 11th Fund. Clothing, food, flashlights, tools, and other equipment were collected at schools, churches, temples, YMCA's, offices, and stores all throughout New York City and in other towns and cities from Long Island to Los Angeles. Local television news reported items that were needed by the rescue workers along with items that were no longer needed thanks to an overflow of generosity. There was even a need for dog food for the dogs that were working at the former site of the World Trade Center, helping to sniff the grounds looking for people trapped in the wreckage.

Kids also pitched in and helped by raising money and goods for the families of the victims and the rescue crews. Students in the Austin, Texas school system held fundraisers, which brought in over $70,000. They also put together care packages for the rescue workers. In Newton, Massachusetts, third grade students held a yard sale and raised $1,000 for the relief effort. The money was also matched by a community bank in the area. In nearby Falmouth, Massachusetts, public school students brought in red, white, and blue yarn and put it in baskets where other students could make the yarn into bracelets and leave a donation for the Red Cross. Down south, in Florida's Winter Park High School, students teamed up to give money to local citizens who were affected by the attacks. They also organized a candle-lighting ceremony

What could you do

to try to help someone directly affected by the September 11th terrorist attacks?

Volunteerism can take many forms. After the September 11th disaster, these children from a Tennessee school collected stuffed animals to send to children who lost parents in the attack.

in the local stadium, which took place after a football game. At the Frank P. Long Intermediate School on Long Island, students ran bake sales and tag sales to raise money to donate to local families who had lost loved ones. In New York City, numerous school children were the recipients of letters written by fellow students at schools in other states, all sending their wishes, support, and prayers. Classes in Manhattan's Kremer Street Elementary School sponsored a project called Kids 4 Kids. The students collected toys to give to children who had lost a parent in the World Trade Center attack. Students in the school donated toys that were special to them or went out and bought new toys with their own money. The students also made personal, heartwarming gift cards to accompany the toys

Garage sales, toy and clothing drives, bake sales, car washes, school talent shows, breakfasts for the community, and numerous creative ways to raise funds were part of the September and October school year in every town and city. Proceeds were sent to one, or several, of the many places set up to collect donations for those in need after the attacks. But, it didn't end there. As the holidays approached, people continued to embrace the spirit of giving, through volunteering and community service activities. The terrible events of September 11th had awakened people to the need to help others, not only in harrowing times, but everyday. In fact, a national poll taken by the America's Promise website, five months

Can you describe

a fundraising activity that you could organize to raise money for the victims and survivors of the World Trade Center attacks?

after the attacks showed that 67% of the people who responded had maintained their increased volunteering time since September 11th. People had started volunteering because of this tragedy and had apparently continued doing for others.

Volunteers Needed!

■ Ten-year-old Daniel had never volunteered in a homeless shelter before, but he promised his older sisters he would try to help out. His first day on the job, he helped his sisters pour soup and hand out meals to a line of homeless people who had come in for lunch. The city had seen many layoffs and more and more people were out of jobs, making places like this one more crowded than ever before. Daniel could not help but stare at the people coming in, wondering how they would get by on little or no money and very little to eat. Marie, his oldest sister, could see that he was uncomfortable. She took him aside and suggested that he might be more comfortable doing something else. Daniel had always enjoyed drawing and was rather good at it. So, to help brighten up the atmosphere, Daniel began some drawings for the shelter. Since they might not get noticed on the walls, he suggested using them as placemats on the trays at dinner. After creating six drawings Daniel hit the local copy shop and ran off a hundred copies. Soon, his original artwork covered the dull gray trays. Daniel saw several people look at the placemats and smile. They felt as if someone had taken time to brighten their day ever so slightly. It was Daniel's way of making a small contribution.

Volunteers aren't only needed in times of crisis. Community organizations like homeless shelters need help year-round to provide those in need with food, clothing, and a place to stay.

It doesn't take a horrible tragedy like that of September 11th to create a need for volunteers. There is always a need to help others in your community. Doing community service can range from helping an elderly person with chores on a one-to-one basis, to collecting clothes, food, or other goods for many people in need. It can mean lending an ear to someone who wants to talk or reading to a sick child in a hospital bed. Poverty, aging, and illness create situations whereby people need the help of others. Very often, these people do not have a family to turn to, or their family has deserted them. Sometimes high medical bills or the loss of a job is the reason why people need your assistance. At other times, natural disasters, such as floods, hurricanes, or tornados have created a situation where families need food, shelter, or medical assistance and cannot get it without help. No matter how people find themselves in difficult situations, there are many individuals out there who can be helped through the **generosity** and good deeds of volunteers, such as you.

Volunteering is certainly not a new concept. It did not begin in recent generations. All throughout history, people have wanted to pitch in and do their share to help others who may be less fortunate. It is one reason why, unlike the dinosaurs, human beings have endured. Ironically, wartime, when there is fighting and killing, has often been a time where there has been the greatest outpouring of volunteers. During wars, volunteers have helped roll bandages, treat wounded soldiers, entertain and boost the morale of the troops, and gather supplies back home. In peacetime, people have also looked out for those who need help during difficult times. For example, during the **Great Depression** of the 1930s in the United States, soup kitchens were manned by thousands of volunteers helping to feed many of the millions of people who were out of work. Serious diseases and **epidemics**, such as small pox, influenza, and cholera, which affected this country during the early to mid 20th century, and the more recent HIV epidemic, have also brought people together to help those who are ill and raise money to fight the disease.

How would it feel

to help sick children by volunteering in a hospital?

Kids have always played a part in volunteering. For example, children helped raise the funds to build the pedestal on which the Statue of Liberty stands. During the 19th century, children volunteered in the dangerous mission of providing food to the slaves who used the **Underground Railroad** to escape the grip of slavery. The Boy Scouts, Girl Scouts, and the Junior Red Cross were all formed to help young people learn about, and take an active role in, doing good deeds for others.

Today, children and teens are frequently seen helping in homeless shelters, community centers, senior centers, and in places such as the Ronald McDonald Houses, which are homes for seriously ill children. Classes in many cities and towns have gone on school outings to clean up parks, paint over graffiti, and help beautify their neighborhoods. School sponsored letter-writing campaigns to government officials have also made a difference in local laws or government activities. This, too, is a form of volunteering by getting involved in an issue of local, or even global, importance. In fact, a letter from a ten-year-old girl, Samantha Reed Smith, to Yuri Andropov, the leader of the Soviet Union, made the headlines in 1982. She asked him not to have a war with the United States. The letter showed the world how one young girl could make a difference, as she spoke up to help make sure there was peace between these two great nations.

Besides helping other people, it's important to understand how volunteering helps you . . . yes, you. Until you go out and volunteer, it's very hard to understand the marvelous feeling one gets when you truly help someone else. There is a special good feeling that comes with volunteering. It's called a "warm

Can you describe

how volunteering could help you, as well as the person you are helping?

Keeping our communities clean and free of graffiti is another way volunteers can help. Volunteer projects throughout the country are currently beautifying neighborhoods, creating community gardens, and cleaning up local parks.

and fuzzy" feeling because it makes you feel good deep down inside.

Helping others is also cathartic, which means it is a way of helping yourself deal with your own problems. It lets a person get away from his or her own problems for a while and focus on the concerns of others. Volunteering may even help you put your own problems into better perspective. One young boy stopped feeling sorry for himself after not making his school basketball team when he went with his church group to donate gifts to children in a local hospital. After leaving the hospital he remarked, "I guess not making the team really isn't the worst thing in the world."

In addition, volunteering is a great way to explore new talents of your own. You may never have thought you were much of a singer, but when you sang holiday songs for elderly people in a nursing home, you realized you enjoyed singing and might even want to take voice lessons. Most people have hidden talents that they never get the opportunity to use. Volunteering offers an opportunity to explore those other talents. For example, if you love drawing, what better way to illustrate your drawings than to design posters or fliers for an upcoming fundraiser? Perhaps you are a whiz at designing costumes. Here's your chance to design costumes for the local theater group version of the play

What are your talents and how could you use them in a volunteer situation?

"Grease." Maybe, throughout school, you've always been nicknamed the "class clown." You use your "clowning skills" in a productive way and entertain children in a pediatric ward.

Besides utilizing some of your other skills, volunteering can help you achieve some of your goals. For instance, if you are looking to stay in shape, you might volunteer in a situation that has you running around, or lifting and "working out." You might want a pet but know nothing about taking care of one. Volunteering to work at a local animal shelter will help the animals get proper care, and provide you with on-the-job training for taking care of a pet

Volunteering time to your community not only helps others, it can help you too. Donating your time to an after-school athletics program can help keep you active and healthy.

of your own. You can learn a lot while volunteering. You can also meet many other people with interests similar to yours. If you are cleaning up a neighborhood park with 200 other people, you'll find that most of these people, just like you, are concerned about the environment. You can establish new relationships while making a difference environmentally. Many friendships develop while doing volunteer work because you are all working on the same project and for the same reasons. Sometimes family members volunteer together and get to know each other in a whole new way, as partners working together as a team, rather than in the usual roles of parents and children or siblings.

And finally, while you should volunteer for all of the reasons above, one more reason to volunteer is that when you seek out colleges to attend and look for jobs in the future, volunteering shows that you have an interest in helping others and doing community service. This always works well in your favor. In fact, you may get school credits for your volunteer work while also gaining valuable life experience.

Working
with Others

Tanya never really liked science classes, and now that she was in middle school she did not see how they would be important in her life. Even though science was not her favorite subject she was, however, still getting top grades, as she was in all of her classes. For this reason, one of the school counselors asked her if she would like to get involved in a program in which some of the students were tutoring fourth and fifth graders. Tanya agreed to sign up. What she didn't know was that there was a shortage of science tutors. She would have much preferred tutoring English, or even Math. Then she met Mark, a nine-year-old who was in a special program for children with learning disabilities. At first she thought it was going to be a real chore trying to help Mark learn a subject she didn't even like. But after a few weeks, she saw Mark making tremendous progress in science. She actually started to look forward to their appointments. By the end of the term, she not only had helped him learn all about how electricity works, but she also had a greater appreciation for science herself. In fact, the

Volunteering your time as a tutor can help you learn about yourself as well. Working with others, although requiring effort and patience, can be a mutually rewarding experience.

following year, Tanya asked if she could join the program again and even requested tutoring in science. Helping Mark not only had an impact on him, but it apparently made a difference for Tanya as well.

One of the most rewarding ways to volunteer is to work directly with other people. From coaching young children in a sports program to helping in a senior center, there are many possibilities. Working with others opens the door to learning about many different kinds of people. Also, as in Tanya's case, it opens the door to learning more about yourself.

Volunteering to work with other people takes some extra effort on your part. First, you have to communicate with people in clear manner. This may mean speaking another language, using sign language, or simply talking with younger children in a way that will maintain their interest. Second, you need to win the respect of whomever you are helping, by treating them in a respectful manner. Third, since you are older, but not yet a "grown up," younger kids may look to you as a role model or as their leader. It is important that you don't let them down. They may take whatever you tell them very seriously.

If you knew a younger student was failing a class, would you volunteer to help him or her get better grades?

Older kids who tutor or coach young children, usually find that when they make learning a fun experience, the children are more receptive. Young children are a lot of fun to work with but you need to have great patience. You can't expect more from them than they can give. If you're fourteen and helping a group of six-year-olds learn to play basketball at a local youth center, you must remember that most of them will not be the next Kobe Bryant . . . in fact, most of them won't be very good. Therefore, you need to have realistic expectations whenever you work with young children, whether it's at sports or helping them with schoolwork. Always be aware of each child's abilities and limitations, and don't be pushy. If you take it all way too seriously, the kids won't have fun. Remember, think "Fun."

Volunteering with senior citizens is another way to work directly with people in your community. This may mean helping a senior get his or her groceries or running errands for them. It may also mean simply spending time talking, playing a board game, or looking at photo albums. These "friendly visits" require you to establish a good rapport and be a good listener.

Often seniors have many stories they want to tell you. Remember, the things you are familiar with may not be the same as that which they will talk about. Therefore, you have a **generation gap,** meaning you were born at very different times and relate to the world in different ways. This presents you with a wonderful opportunity to explain some of the things going on in your life while learning about what the world was like when these individuals were younger.

> **What would you talk about** with an elderly person who just wanted you to keep them company?

When working with older people, you need to be patient and understanding. Someone who has been active throughout his or her life may be frustrated that he or she has slowed down because of age. It can be difficult for someone who is used to doing everything for him or herself to need to rely on someone else to help them. You need to help in a kind and gentle way and not be patronizing. Once you establish a good relationship with a senior, your visit might be one of the brightest parts of his or her week . . . as well as yours.

You can also help people through working with the homeless. A sad reality of society today is that there are many people without a place to call home. Drug addiction, physical and mental illnesses, and unemployment are among the reasons why these people have become homeless. You are not there to ask a lot of questions or to try and solve all of a homeless person's problems (even if you wish you could). Helping those who are homeless

It's a sad fact that seniors are often neglected in our society. By volunteering at a senior center, you can build productive relationships with older adults who have a lot of interesting experiences to share.

means respecting their rights as people, as well as their privacy. They may have very few possessions, but those that they have are very important to them.

Before helping the homeless, it may be a good idea to stand and watch from a distance for an hour during your first visit to a shelter. This will get you past the initial uncomfortable feeling you may have when you first arrive. You may not want to stay and work, but can be helpful by delivering groceries, clothing, games, or toys. If it is the holiday season you might provide holiday decorations. There is a lot you can do to make the life of a homeless person or family a little brighter.

Would you be comfortable

volunteering in a soup kitchen or homeless shelter?

There are many other ways to help others directly, such as reading to someone who is blind or doing chores for someone who is injured or disabled. If another person needs help in some manner and you can provide that help as a service or good dead, then you are acting as a volunteer.

Community Service

■ They were called the Green Rangers—they were not a base-ball or a hockey team, but a group of neighborhood kids aged 11-16 who helped beautify their western Pennsylvania town. Factories and businesses had replaced much of the greenery with big buildings and storefronts over the years. The children had seen photos of their town, which had been taken twenty years earlier, and saw how much nicer the town looked with trees and plants. They decided to team up every spring and plant trees and flowers along the sides of the highways that crossed through town, and in the neighborhood parks that were turning brown from lack of care and attention. They wanted to make their town look like it once did.

Today, the kids who made up the original Green Rangers have grown up, but those who are still living in the town today take pride in the fact that they helped make over a town from gray steel and brown grass to healthy trees and green grass.

If you like working outdoors, you can volunteer at a community garden, zoo, or wildlife center. You'll not only be helping out—you'll also learn a lot about the plants and animals that share our world.

Parks, zoos, libraries, schools, community centers, and street fairs can all use the services of volunteers. There are possibilities for **community service** in every neighborhood.

If you enjoy the great outdoors, you might want to volunteer to plant or help beautify a park or garden. All you will need is some stamina, a little sun screen (or at least a hat) and some old clothes that you don't mind getting dirty. Planting and gardening are fun activities to do with a group of people. However, if gardening isn't for you, or allergies keep you at a safe distance from plants, you might simply want to do clean up work. Every neighborhood has at least one playground that can use a facelift. From painting benches to cleaning up graffiti to picking up trash, you can be part of a valuable team. A ten-year-old girl who helped clean a park in Manhattan said "It's more fun cleaning up a park than cleaning my room. More people will get to use the park than will ever visit my room."

Zoos are also great places for doing community service, too. Usually, handling the animals is left up to those people with more professional "animal" training. However, you can learn a lot about the animals by watching and assisting. You may also be put in a position where you can answer questions from visitors or help guide tours. This will

Can you describe

the type of job you might want to do at a local wildlife center or zoo?

generally require you to take some classes to learn more about the animals and how they are cared for. It's to your benefit to pay close attention and learn as much as you can if you are going to help visitors enjoy their experience at a zoo, **wildlife center,** or an aquarium.

Every community also has several **institutions,** such as museums, post offices, or libraries that are run by the state or federal government. Many of these places do not have enough money to hire all the help they really need.

Libraries, for example, are often understaffed. Putting books back on the shelves, helping with a used book sale, or providing information for young readers can all be volunteer opportunities in a local library. Other ways of volunteering at a library are to help raise money through fundraising drives and special events, and to promote the library in the community.

Community centers, church groups, synagogues, or other gathering places within your area are also often busy trying to raise money to help people in the community who are less fortunate. Many community centers sponsor events such as street fairs for which they will need people to man booths or tables. Keep in mind that when volunteering in a community setting of any kind, the volunteering jobs are run in a certain manner.

What would you do

if you discovered a better way to do a job you volunteered for at a community center?

All volunteers need to follow the rules and guidelines so that everything is done the same way. Volunteers cannot just do what they want. If someone has an idea for a new way of doing something, he or she should make a suggestion to the person in charge.

Believe it or not, you might even return to your school after school hours or on weekends to do volunteer work. Many schools have after-school activity programs. You could help other students learn to play chess, roller blade, or do art projects. The school library may also need volunteers, or the gym may require someone to put the equipment back in the storage room. School volunteers at one New Jersey public school serve snacks to parents at PTA meetings and family events on evenings and weekends. The money they raise

Volunteer opportunities are often as close as your own school. School libraries often need help re-shelving books, updating magazines, or planning special events.

goes to help support the after-school activities. Other grade schools all over the country have environmental programs where students are asked to bring in empty cans and bottles that they find for deposit. The money raised from collecting the bottles and cans goes for school trips or other student activities.

You might also take a volunteer role by discovering an issue in you your neighborhood that needs to be addressed. For example, there may be a very dangerous intersection where there have been several accidents.

Therefore, a traffic light may be needed. Writing letters to politicians or having people sign a petition to correct something that you believe should be changed is another way of doing community service for a worthwhile cause. Students at one middle school started a petition, which would allow someone not born in the United States, but a U.S. citizen for 25 years, to run for President of the United States. Students got hundreds of signatures and sent the petition to Washington, D.C. While it is not very likely that this petition will change the legal guidelines for running for president, it may be the first step in making other people aware of this law. A local petition in a small town, however, might get enough signatures to have a law changed.

Clubs, associations, and charitable organizations are also great places in which to do community service. Your parents may belong to a club or organization that can use your services. Abby, age nine, went with her dad when the parent-based organization he belongs to took a day trip to the state capital to meet with lawmakers about laws affecting children. She even spoke up in the meetings and expressed her concerns about issues that children faced.

Local meetings of groups and associations can also need volunteers to help at meetings and social events, such as serving refreshments at meetings, helping to stuff envelopes, or making fliers to promote an upcoming event. Charitable groups and organizations, as well as your school, church, temple, community center, and local library all sponsor fundraisers. The money raised may be

Can you describe

an activity or event that you would want to organize to raise money for a club or organization?

used directly to help repair the school or build a new roof for the church, or it may be donated to a larger charitable organization. Following the September 11th tragedy, the Red Cross, United Way, Salvation Army, and many other well-known organizations collected millions of dollars to help families of the victims through local fund raisers all over the country.

While fundraising can be very simple, such as passing a collection plate around, it is frequently centered around an activity that you can be a part of, such as a school play, bake sale, garage sale, car wash, dance marathon, basketball game, etc. Fundraising efforts can bring you closer to a good cause, such as raising money for children fighting cancer, without having to do volunteer work in a hospital or a place where you might not feel comfortable. It's another very important manner of volunteering. Money is always needed to fight diseases, help feed and clothe people who are less fortunate, or repair and beautify the neighborhood. Volunteers collecting money for charity need to be responsible and know how much money they have collected. They need to have a safe place to put collected funds and one person in charge of handling all the money collected by other volunteers. If an organization has a treasurer, you can be sure he or she will end up with the responsibility of collecting the money and sending it to the charity or other group that it is being sent to.

Selling items, such as magazines in a magazine drive (whereby students sell magazine subscriptions from a selection offered through the school), can also raise money. Often a school, or an organization sponsoring the drive, will offer a prize to the winner as an **incentive** to sell more magazines and raise more money. You're probably familiar with the famous Girl Scout Cookies, which have been sold for many years to raise funds. Today, gift-wrapping paper is a popular fund raising item, often sold during the holiday season.

Selling something, whether it's cookies, magazines, or holiday wrapping paper, requires that you present your product clearly, explain some of the benefits to the potential buyer and give them the opportunity to think about making a purchase. You should also make it clear why you are selling the products. Becky, an eleven-year-old salesperson for her school, stumbled upon a customer who thought it was terrible that the school was asking young children to sell magazines to raise money. Becky, and her mom, pointed out that kids not only enjoyed getting involved in helping their school, but were also learning about sales, interacting with other people, and raising money for a good cause. The person complaining didn't understand that volunteers usually enjoy what they do and gain emotional rewards for doing it.

A specific time and place are set up to collect donations of food, clothing, books, toys or whatever it is you are collecting. The volunteers will then sort through the items to make sure everything meets the needs of the particular drive. If, for example, you were collecting toys for toddlers and found that someone brought in a toy for kids 7 to 9 years old, you would

What would you say

to someone who wanted to make a donation that didn't meet the needs of your particular drive?

either not accept this donation, or you might put it in a separate pile and later donate it elsewhere. Likewise, only canned food can be collected for a food drive to make sure it will stay fresh. Therefore, not everything can be collected in a donation drive.

Communities often need volunteers to help raise funds for a particular project or relief effort. After the September 11th disaster, many communities organized bake sales, clothing drives, and sales of patriotic ribbons to bring in needed money and supplies.

When collecting items, you can take them to a larger charitable organization, such as the Red Cross, who will distribute them for you, or you can sometimes deliver items yourself. One of the most rewarding moments in volunteering is when you do have the pleasure of actually handing out the items that you have collected in a donation drive. Putting a Christmas present in the hand of a child in a hospital bed is a very rewarding volunteer job. Your pay is the smiles on the faces of the children. That's what volunteering is all about, bringing good feelings and comfort to others.

Choosing a Volunteer Opportunity that is Right for You

■ Carolyn fidgeted nervously before her big interview. She wanted so much to work at the children's museum. She had gone there many times with her parents since she was three years old. Now, at thirteen, she read that the museum was looking for volunteers to help run the gift shop and the play activities. Today she was meeting with the head of the museum. A month ago, she thought she could volunteer at a local clinic for children infected with HIV, but realized that she was not helpful because if was too upsetting for her. She hoped this would be a more comfortable place for her to do community service.

After a short wait, the woman who ran the volunteer division of the museum met with Carolyn and asked her why she wanted to work at the museum and what skills she possessed that would make her a good volunteer. Talking slowly and choosing her words carefully, Carolyn explained that she loved working with children and had helped out in an after school program with younger kids. She also explained that she had been to the museum many times, so she was very familiar with it. In addition, she mentioned that she was always on time for school and rarely ever absent. She also explained that she would be a good volunteer because she liked helping other people learn new things. Sure enough, Carolyn got the position and started working just one day a week after school. This gave her a chance to see if she liked working at the museum. It also gave the head of the museum an opportunity to see how well Carolyn did on the job. Carolyn turned out to be exactly the kind of volunteer the museum needed.

Community service is more than just showing up and being ready to lend a hand. It means making a commitment to doing a job, whether it's for just one day or for several hours every week. If you want to find a place where you can volunteer often, it's a good idea to start by looking at several possible volunteer opportunities and deciding which one would be best for you. For example, if you are uncomfortable or nervous around people who are ill, then a hospital would not be the best place for you. Remember, not every volunteer opportunity is for everyone. Don't feel guilty if one opportunity isn't right for you . . . there are plenty of others.

Along with wanting to feel comfortable, volunteers should look to work in an area of personal interest or help work for a cause in which they believe. When you enter into a volunteer situation, you want to help make something better or see something change. There is a goal to volunteering. You want to see the buildings in your neighborhood look clean and fresh without graffiti, or the cats and dogs in an animal shelter receive good care. You might want to simply bring a smile to the face of someone who is sick or want to raise money to help find a cure for an illness.

It's important to choose a volunteer activity that's right for you—like working at a recycling center because you want to protect the environment. If you like working with people, you might volunteer at a senior center, hospital, or homeless shelter.

People usually choose a volunteer opportunity for a reason. You might recall something that had and impact on your life. For example, Kirby Puckett, a former major league baseball star for the Minnesota Twins, now volunteers a great deal of his time helping the **Glaucoma** Foundation. He is involved with this organization because glaucoma, a serious vision-related disease, forced him to retire from major league baseball. Now he wants to let others know that they should have their eyes tested. Likewise, ten-year-old Angie helps her parents who volunteer at an adoption support group because she was adopted as a child, and like her parents, feels grateful that the support group helped them become a family. You may just hate the fact that kids can't go swimming in

Can you describe

something that has happened in your life that would make you want to volunteer for a specific cause?

the neighborhood lake anymore because of pollution and want to help pass around a petition to have it cleaned out. If you are very concerned about the environment, you might also consider helping in a recycling center. There are so many volunteer opportunities available that you can usually find one that you feel passionate about.

You will also want to match your skills to those that are needed at the place at which you are looking to volunteer. Some jobs require volunteers to work with their hands, some need people who speak another language, while others need volunteers who are good at using the computer. One job may simply need someone who is friendly and outgoing while another may be perfect for someone who is shy because it involves more research and less communication with other people. When planning to volunteer it's highly recommended that you consider what you do well.

While you are scouting for the volunteer opportunities that interest you, keep in mind that the people running homeless shelters, soup kitchens, libraries, community centers, senior centers, wildlife centers, charities, and medical centers will also be evaluating you. In general, volunteers will not need all the **credentials** it might take to land a paying job, but a level of skill is needed to handle any volunteer position. You will usually be asked, in an interview, what qualities you have that will make you the right volunteer for the job. It's a good idea to learn what volunteers do at the location where you are looking to volunteer. You might even know someone who has worked in a similar place who can fill you in on what it is like working there as a volunteer on a regular basis.

Can you describe

the skills that would make you a good volunteer?

In addition to learning about the volunteer opportunities,

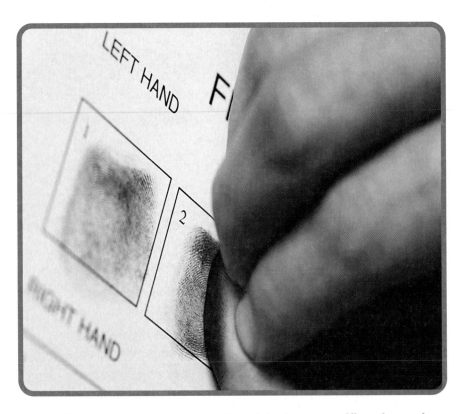

Remember that some volunteer jobs have specific rules and requirements. In some states, people who work with children are required to be fingerprinted. Be sure you find out what the rules are and respect them.

there may be specific requirements necessary for doing a volunteer job. For example, people working with children, in certain states, are required to be finger-printed. Some states require volunteers to be tested for certain illnesses, such as tuberculosis, before working with seniors. A tetanus shot may be required before working at a recycling center.

Combining your skills and abilities with the needs of the job will help you find the best volunteer opportunity for you. An orientation, training session, or even several weeks of classes may be required to learn a volunteering job. This learning can take ten minutes if you're being trained to clean up the playground or ten weeks of classes if you

How would you decide which volunteer opportunity is right for you?

are going to conduct tours of the local aquarium. The more information you are expected to pass along to other people, the more you'll have to learn. Consider how much learning you are ready to do before taking on a volunteer position.

Besides seeking out community service opportunities of interest, volunteers also need to consider the practical elements of getting involved. Most organizations and associations will want a regular time commitment. Look at your schedule closely before committing to too many hours each week. You may want to start off with a simple task that requires only two hours a week to test out the waters and see if you like working in the environment. If you are comfortable, and realize you still have plenty of time to get your schoolwork done, see your friends, and participate in other activities, then you might ask for a task that takes six or seven hours a week. "I started with just a few hours once a week after school," says 14-year-old Kenya, who reads to the children at the library reading room. "Now I read to them three days a week. It just got to be fun. It doesn't affect my time to do homework either because I have a chance to read on the bus home from the library."

Also, volunteers need to remember to include the time spent traveling to and from a volunteer opportunity and what transportation they will take. If you are volunteering for an hour a day but need two hours by bus to get to and from the location, you may not have made a good choice. You might look for a volunteer opportunity closer to your home or school. One of the leading reasons why many people do not volunteer is because they are concerned that it will take too much of their time. Volunteering close to home can help solve that problem. Also rearranging your schedule can usually clear a little bit of time for volunteering. Sometimes it's as simple as skipping two or three hours of television each week. "I used to hang out in the playground almost everyday then walk home from school" says 15-year-old Pedro. "Now, two days a week I skip hanging out and take the bus home so I can help out at the church down the block. They're building a new after school center for younger kids and I think it's important. I have three younger brothers and they'll have a place to go."

What would you do to rearrange your schedule so you had time to volunteer?

There are many factors that go into deciding what the best volunteer opportunity is for you. Look at the possibilities and decide if you want to be a part of the team. For example, does it seem like a place where you will fit in? Will the project be stimulating enough for you or will you be bored? What are the other volunteers like? How will you get there? What is the time commitment? Get as many answers as you can before making a commitment.

Three Volunteering Reminders

1. Part of doing any type of community service or volunteering in any manner is getting along with the other volunteers. Everyone involved should show each other respect. If you disagree with someone, remember to politely criticize the ideas, not the person.

   "I don't think we should run the book sale next weekend because too many people will be out of town" is criticizing the idea to run the book sale on that weekend. But, responding with "Fred, next weekend is no good, you always have such stupid ideas" is not addressing the problem but criticizing the person.

   All volunteers are working for a worthy cause and want that positive feeling that comes with doing the hard work. Therefore, you don't want to rain on their parade.

2. Once you start working on a project, you will discover that all volunteers do not work at the same pace. Therefore, you may need to pitch in and help someone who is moving along more slowly on his or her part of the project. Not everyone will do an equal amount of work. Volunteering is not a competition; it is giving of yourself in whatever manner you can.

3. If you decide that you no longer want to be involved in a project, finish the work you are doing and let the person in charge know that you are not going to continue. Don't just vanish since others are counting on you.

Starting Your Own Volunteer Project

■ Mark, age 13, and his younger sister Carolyn, age 8, were very upset by the events of September 11th. They wanted to do something to help raise money for the families who lost loved ones. Since Carolyn and her mom enjoyed baking cupcakes and lemonade was pretty easy to make, they decided to open a refreshment stand between 3 and 5 o'clock in the playground behind the school, which was very busy once school let out. They sat down and had a meeting to decide how much to charge and where in the schoolyard they would set up the stand. Carolyn's mom checked with the school to see if it would be all right. She then called the local chapter of the Red Cross to see if they could donate the money to the victims and survivors of the September 11th tragedy. The school was fine with the idea and the Red Cross assured her that they would gladly take all the donations that came in for this worthy cause.

Then, Mark had a patriotic idea. He rummaged through his closet and came out holding a shoebox. He and his sister had been to a party for the Fourth of July a couple years earlier. Little plastic toothpicks with flags on the top were sticking out of all the deserts at the party. He remembered how they collected the little flags from all the other kids who didn't want them or had left them on the table. There were nearly 100 of them in the shoebox. So, they washed off the toothpicks in hot water and added a patriotic touch to the first couple batches of cupcakes, which sold more like hotcakes. Interestingly, this time the kids who got the flags were not so quick to give them to someone else or toss them aside. After September 11th, everyone seemed to want to hold onto their flags and display them.

Following the events of September 11th, many people took it upon themselves to come up with ways to raise money to help. Schools, businesses, and associations all thought up their own ways of raising money. When tornados, hurricanes, or floods destroy a community, disaster relief organizations act fast and gather the money and items necessary to help victims who have been affected.

To start a volunteer project, however, you need not wait for a disaster to strike. You only need to look around and determine what you can do to make life better for someone else, or for your community. Next you need to figure out how you can help. Does the situation require that you roll up your sleeves and do work? Can you help directly by cleaning up, painting, or building something? Would raising money be the best way to help? Could you collect food or clothing donations?

If you are raising funds, you need to determine what you can do that will inspire people to donate money. Volunteer groups try hard to come up with fundraising ideas that can be done without spending much money. Garage sales, bake

There are lots of ways to put your own volunteer projects into action. With the help of parents and schools, kids have set up their own garage sales, bake sales, magazine drives, bike-a-thons, and other fundraising events.

sales, magazine drives, dance marathons, walk-a-thons or bike-a-thons, county fairs, sporting events, and other activities are ways in which you can combine your skills with those of others to raise funds for a cause. There are numerous possibilities. One high school challenged their teachers to an Olympics, where they picked five events to play against the teachers, including basketball and volleyball. Several schools report

What would you do

to spread the word about a school fundraiser if you were put in charge of promotion?

success with art shows or talent shows where they charge admission to see works of art or to be entertained by the best talent the students have to offer. Whatever you come up with, you need to find a place and set a time and date. Consider several possibilities since your first choice may not work out. Also, take into account all possible problems that may occur with the time and place. For example a charity basketball game will not work at 6 P.M. if the gym has another activity taking place at 8:30.

Make sure to give yourself plenty of time to work out *all* the details. It's important to think about every task that needs to get done ahead of time. Even doing something as simple as a car wash means having buckets, hoses, water, soap, squeegees, and plenty of rags on hand, plus a place to wash the cars. It also means putting up signs, deciding on a price, setting a date and a time, having something in which to collect money and making sure you have enough people on hand to help. You may also need to come up with a rain date. Write it all down and decide who will be the best person to handle each task.

Don't forget to let a lot of people get involved. At first it's tempting to try to do almost everything yourself. The reality is, you'll have a lot of work just making sure everything else is getting done and everyone is doing his or her jobs. Assign roles to each person who wants to get involved and don't be afraid to let people try new tasks, even if they haven't done them before. Remember, everyone needs encouragement and sometimes someone new will have an innovative way of doing an important job. There's usually one person who will volunteer to do five jobs at once. While their intentions are good, it's generally not in the best interest of the project to give one person more than you think they can handle. Spreading the work around allows more volunteers to get involved. Also, if one person does

When planning a volunteer project, be sure you have all the details covered. You'll need to collect the supplies you'll need and publicize the event so people know about it.

not do his or her assigned task, or is working slowly, it is easy to pitch in and help. However, if one person has five tasks and falls behind on all of them or does not do four of the five, the whole project suffers.

Instead of doing something to raise money, volunteers often work at collection drives. The Salvation Army, formed in the 1820s, has become well known for collecting items such as clothing for people in need. Before you collect anything, however, make sure you have a place to which you can donate the items. Check with a local shelter or hospital and see if they will accept coats, food, clothes, toys, or whatever you are collecting. In fact, you may ask them what is most needed. One New York City children's organization held a toothpaste drive for overseas orphanages where children did not have toothpaste. People donated hundreds of unopened tubes of toothpaste that were sent to the orphanages.

Can you describe

the guidelines and rules you would establish if you were put in charge of a clothing drive?

When running a collection drive, you need to find a central location and make sure to spread the word about what you are collecting and when you are collecting it. Also, be specific about what type of items you are looking to collect. For example, a toy drive for needy children is a wonderful idea. However, you need to consider what age children these toys or games will be going to. You'll have other considerations too, such as whether you will accept used toys which could have broken parts, if you are looking for people to bring new unwrapped toys. There are usually guidelines set up in advance of a donation drive. You might clearly state that you want new toys for toddlers, since that is the age group to whom you will be delivering them. You might also specify that you do not want toy guns or weapons. Set up a few guidelines, or rules, for any volunteer project you undertake.

Whatever type of volunteering activity you are looking to organize, you should start by sitting down at the computer, or with pen and paper, and making a long list of what tasks need to be done and what guidelines you will need to set up. Try to think about all the possibilities and ask friends and family if they can think of anything you forgot.

Many of the volunteer opportunities discussed throughout this book, such as reading to the blind or visiting children in a hospital, can be organized by simply offering your services. You can organize a one-day project

Whether at home or school, a computer can help you list the supplies you need and learn about community guidelines that will make your volunteer effort a success.

or start a volunteer group that meets often. Just as one local park cleanup group called themselves the Green Rangers, another group might be the Young Hospital Cadets. Whatever name you come up with, you can start a volunteer group with a specific goal or purpose.

A group called Kids Cheering Kids was formed in Los Gatos, California, when a five-year-old boy named John told his mom that he felt very lucky and wanted other kids to feel as lucky as he was. He asked his mom, *"Why can't kids help kids?"* Now, thanks to the work of John and his mom, Kids Cheering Kids is a busy non-profit organization for kids aged five and

> **What would you do**
>
> **to start a volunteer group in your neighborhood or community?**

over that helps other kids. They visit other children in the a local recovery center, go for outings with kids in homeless shelters, help tutor kids who are having a hard time academically, and do other activities.

Charitable organizations like the Red Cross or volunteer groups like the **United Service Organization (USO)**, all started because someone wanted to begin volunteering and took the first step at organizing a volunteer group. You can do it too.

Once a volunteer group is established, they often wear clothing, such as t-shirts or hats, to promote themselves and the work that they do. The Guardian Angels, a New York City based volunteer safety patrol who were originally formed to protect subway riders, became known for their red berets, Guardian Angel t-shirts, and red jackets. Today, they have a day proclaimed in their honor by former New York City Mayor Rudolph Giuliani. In time, a volunteer group can gain attention in their area or region and be called upon to help wherever they are needed. Of course, this will only happen after the group has proven that they are dedicated to working hard to help others.

Perhaps you can prove you dedication to helping others by starting a volunteer organization of your own.

Glossary

Command center — a central location from which the main operations, or tasks being done, are managed and key decisions are made.

Credentials — a listing of past skills, experiences, and education in an area of study.

Epidemic — a contagious disease that spreads very quickly and affects many people.

Generation Gap — different ways of viewing the world based on the time period in which a person was born. For example, one generation may be familiar with a record player, while another generation is more familiar with a CD player.

Generosity — the act of giving to others.

Great Depression — the time period after the stock market crashed in 1929. The price of stock in many companies fell and investors all over America lost a great deal of money. As a result, for the next several years, millions of people could not find jobs and had little to eat.

Ground Zero — the name of the former site of the World Trade Center in lower Manhattan.

Incentives — rewards for doing activities, or reasons to be motivated to do a good job.

Institutions — established organizations such as schools, libraries or museums, most often run by the government and through donations.

Recession — a period of time in which businesses across the nation, or even the world, are not doing as well as expected. Companies are usually not making much money and many people often lose their jobs.

Glossary

Underground Railroad — not an actual railroad, this was a series of escape routes including secret tunnels and hiding places set up by volunteers who helped slaves escape from the south to the north prior to the Civil War.

United Service Organization (USO) — a non-government, non-profit organization that, for many years, has provided entertainment to American soldiers overseas.

Wildlife Center — similar to a zoo, only there is usually more room for the animals to roam free. It is also a place where conservation and other studies regarding the environment are conducted.

Further Reading

Books:

Duper, Linda Lee. *160 Ways to Help the World: Community Service Projects for Young People.* New York: Facts On File, 1996.

Erlbach, Arlene. *The Kid's Volunteer Book (Kids Ventures).* Minnesota: The Lerner Publishing Group, 1998.

Isler, Claudia. *Volunteering To Help In Your Neighborhood.* New York: Children's Press, 2000.

Organizations and Websites

American Red Cross Youth Services. Since the formation of the Junior Red Cross in 1917, the Red Cross has offered volunteer programs and training for youths. Contact your local chapter for details. *www.redcross.org/services/youth*

JustGive.org offers a Kids Corner featuring plenty of ways kids can help animals, the environment, and other children. You can learn about creative ways to volunteer and search for volunteer opportunities near you. 2782 California Street, 2nd floor, San Francisco, CA 94115. *www.justgive.org*

Volunteer Match is a non-profit website where you can search for volunteer opportunities in your area. There are thousands of listings and they include code letters such as "T" for teens and "K" for kids to let you know if these are open to you. *www.volunteermatch.org*

Youth Volunteer Corps of America is an organization with chapters all over the United States and in various parts of the world. They offer teens from ages 11 to 18 an opportunity to take part in community service projects and be active volunteers. 4600 West 51st Street, Suite 300, Shawnee Mission, KS 66205. *www.yvca.org*

Further Reading

Youth Service America (YSA) is a resource center that includes over 200 organizations and many programs designed to support youth volunteering. YSA sponsors National Youth Service Day and the President's Student Service Awards, which recognizes volunteers, ages 5 through 25, who contribute over 50 hours of service a year. The YSA website includes SERVEnet.org can locate volunteer opportunities by zip code search. 1101 15th Street, Suite 200, Washington, DC 20005 *www.ysa.org*

Index

Index

About the Author

Rich Mintzer is the author of 26 non-fiction books including several for children and teens. He has also written articles for national magazines and material for high school students for the Power to Learn website. He has been a professional writer for nearly 20 years and enjoys writing on many different subjects. Rich is currently living in New York City with his wife and two children.

About the Editor

Marvin Rosen is a licensed clinical psychologist who practices in Media, Pennsylvania. He received his doctorate degree from the University of Pennsylvania in 1961. Since 1963, he has worked with intellectually and emotionally challenged people at Elwyn, Inc. in Pennsylvania, with clinical, administrative, research, and training responsibilities. He also conducts a private practice of psychology. Dr. Rosen has taught psychology at the University of Pennsylvania, Bryn Mawr College, and West Chester University. He has written or edited seven book and numerous professional articles in the areas of psychology, rehabilitation, emotional disturbance, and mental retardation.